MW00424230

NOVENA
TO THE
HOLY GHOST

NOVENA
TO THE
HOLY GHOST

We ought to pray and invoke the Holy Spirit, for each one of us greatly needs His protection and His help. The more a man is deficient in wisdom, weak in strength, borne down with trouble, prone to sin, so ought he the more to fly to Him Who is the never ceasing Fount of Light, Strength, Consolation and Holiness.   —POPE LEO XIII

TAN Books
Charlotte, North Carolina

Imprimi Potest: George J. Collins, C.S.Sp.,
                         Provincial
                         Washington, January 30, 1948

Nihil Obstat: Charles Connors, C.S.Sp., J.C.D.
                         Censor Deputatus

Imprimatur: ✠ Patrick A. O'Boyle, D.D.
                         Archbishop of Washington
                         Washington, March 12, 1948

ISBN: 978-0-89555-262-4

Cover design by Lauren A. Rupar.

Printed and bound in the United States of America.

TAN Books
Charlotte, North Carolina
www.TANBooks.com
2010

Contents

Foreword 1

Act of Consecration to the Holy Ghost 3

Prayer for the Seven Gifts of the
    Holy Ghost 4

First Day 6

Second Day 8

Third Day 10

Fourth Day 12

Fifth Day 14

Sixth Day 16

Seventh Day 18

Eight Day 20

Ninth Day 22

Archconfraternity of the Holy Ghost 24

Foreword

The novena in honor of the Holy Ghost is the oldest of all novenas since it was first made at the direction of Our Lord Himself when He sent His apostles back to Jerusalem to await the coming of the Holy Ghost on the first Pentecost. It is still the only novena officially prescribed by the Church. Addressed to the Third Person of the Blessed Trinity, it is a powerful plea for the light and strength and love so sorely needed by every Christian. To encourage devotion to the Holy Spirit, the Church has enriched this novena with the following indulgences:

The faithful who devoutly assist at the public novena in honor of the Holy Ghost immediately preceding the Feast of Pentecost may gain:

*An indulgence of 10 years on any day of the novena;** *

A plenary indulgence, if they take part in at least five of the exercises, and moreover go to confession, receive Holy Communion and pray for the Holy Father's intention.

Those who make a private novena in honor of the Holy Ghost, either before Pentecost or at any other time in the year, may gain:

An indulgence of 7 years once on any day of their novena;

A plenary indulgence under the usual conditions at the close of the novena; but if a public novena is held, this indulgence is available only to those who are lawfully hindered from taking part in the same.

---

* These indulgences were valid when this booklet was originally published in 1948. The current regulations state that a "partial indulgence" is granted to the faithful who devoutly take part in the pious exercises of a public novena before the feast of Pentecost. (*Enchiridion of Indulgences*, 1968, No. 34). (Partial indulgences are no longer measured in "days" and "years.") —*Publisher*, 2010.

Act of Consecration
to the Holy Ghost

On my knees before the great multitude of heavenly witnesses, I offer myself, soul and body, to You, Eternal Spirit of God. I adore the brightness of Your purity, the unerring keenness of Your justice, and the might of Your love. You are the Strength and Light of my soul. In You I live and move and am. I desire never to grieve You by unfaithfulness to grace and I pray with all my heart to be kept from the smallest sin against You. Mercifully guard my every thought and grant that I may always watch for Your light and listen to Your voice and follow Your gracious inspirations. I cling to You and give myself to You and ask You by Your compassion to watch over me in my weakness. Holding the pierced Feet of Jesus and looking at His Five Wounds and trusting in His Precious Blood and adoring His opened Side and stricken Heart I implore You Adorable Spirit, Helper of my infirmity, so to keep me in Your grace that I may never sin against You. Give me grace, O Holy Ghost, Spirit of the Father and the Son, to say to You always and everywhere "Speak Lord, for Your servant heareth." Amen.

(To be recited daily during the Novena)

Prayer for the Seven Gifts of the Holy Ghost

O Lord Jesus Christ Who, before ascending into Heaven did promise to send the Holy Ghost to finish Your work in the souls of Your Apostles and Disciples, deign to grant the same Holy Spirit to me that He may perfect in my soul the work of Your grace and Your love. Grant me the Spirit of Wisdom that I may despise the perishable things of this world and aspire only after the things that are eternal, the Spirit of Understanding to enlighten my mind with the light of Your divine truth, the Spirit of Counsel that I may ever choose the surest way of pleasing God and gaining Heaven, the Spirit of Fortitude that I may bear my cross with You and that I may overcome with courage all the obstacles that oppose my salvation, the Spirit of Knowledge that I may know God and know myself and grow perfect in the science of the Saints, the Spirit of Piety that I may find the service of God sweet and amiable, the Spirit of Fear that I may be filled with a loving reverence towards God and may dread in any way to displease Him. Mark me, dear Lord, with the sign of Your true disciples and animate me in all things with Your Spirit. Amen.

(To be recited daily during the Novena)

FIRST DAY

Holy Spirit! Lord of light!
From Your clear celestial height,
Your pure beaming radiance give!

The Holy Ghost

Only one thing is important—eternal salvation. Only one thing, therefore, is to be feared—sin. Sin is the result of ignorance, weakness, and indifference. The Holy Ghost is the Spirit of Light, of Strength, and of Love. With His sevenfold gifts He enlightens the mind, strengthens the will, and inflames the heart with love of God. To ensure our salvation we ought to invoke the Divine Spirit daily, for "The Spirit helpeth our infirmity. We know not what we should pray for as we ought. But the Spirit Himself asketh for us."

Prayer

Almighty and eternal God, Who hast vouchsafed to regenerate us by water and the Holy

6

Ghost, and hast given us forgiveness of all sins, vouchsafe to send forth from Heaven upon us Your sevenfold Spirit, the Spirit of Wisdom and Understanding, the Spirit of Counsel and Fortitude, the Spirit of Knowledge and Piety, and fill us with the Spirit of Holy Fear. Amen.

Our Father and Hail Mary ONCE.
Glory be to the Father SEVEN TIMES.
Act of Consecration, Prayer for the Seven Gifts.
(Turn to page 3)

SECOND DAY

Come, Father of the poor!
Come, treasures which endure!
Come, Light of all that live!

The Gift of Fear

The gift of Fear fills us with a sovereign respect for God, and makes us dread nothing so much as to offend Him by sin. It is a fear that arises, not from the thought of Hell, but from sentiments of reverence and filial submission to our heavenly Father. It is the fear that is the beginning of wisdom, detaching us from worldly pleasures that could in any way separate us from God. "They that fear the Lord will prepare their hearts, and in His sight will sanctify their souls."

Prayer

Come, O blessed Spirit of Holy Fear, penetrate my inmost heart, that I may set You, my Lord and God, before my face forever; help me to shun

8

all things that can offend You, and make me worthy to appear before the pure eyes of Your Divine Majesty in Heaven, where You live and reign in the unity of the ever Blessed Trinity, God, world without end. Amen.

Our Father and Hail Mary ONCE.
Glory be to the Father SEVEN TIMES.
Act of Consecration, Prayer for the Seven Gifts.
(Turn to page 3)

THIRD DAY

Thou, of all consolers best,
Visiting the troubled breast,
Dost refreshing peace bestow.

The Gift of Piety

The gift of Piety begets in our hearts a filial affection for God as our most loving Father. It inspires us to love and respect for His sake persons and things consecrated to Him, as well as those who are vested with His authority, His Blessed Mother and the Saints, the Church and its visible Head, our parents and superiors, our country and its rulers. He who is filled with the gift of Piety finds the practice of his religion not a burdensome duty, but a delightful service. Where there is love, there is no labor.

Prayer

Come, O Blessed Spirit of Piety, possess my heart. Enkindle therein such a love for God that

10

I may find satisfaction only in His service, and for His sake lovingly submit to all legitimate authority. Amen.

Our Father and Hail Mary ONCE.
Glory be to the Father SEVEN TIMES.
Act of Consecration, Prayer for the Seven Gifts.
(Turn to page 3)

FOURTH DAY

Thou in toil art comfort sweet;
Pleasant coolness in the heat;
Solace in the midst of woe.

The Gift of Fortitude

By the gift of Fortitude the soul is strengthened against natural fear, and supported to the end in the performance of duty. Fortitude imparts to the will an impulse and energy which move it to undertake without hesitancy the most arduous tasks, to face dangers, to trample under foot human respect, and to endure without complaint the slow martyrdom of even lifelong tribulation. "He that shall persevere unto the end, he shall be saved."

Prayer

Come, O Blessed Spirit of Fortitude, uphold my soul in time of trouble and adversity, sustain my efforts after holiness, strengthen my weakness, give me courage against all the assaults of my enemies, that I may never be overcome and separated from Thee, my God and greatest Good. Amen.

Our Father and Hail Mary ONCE.
Glory be to the Father SEVEN TIMES.
Act of Consecration, Prayer for the Seven Gifts.
(Turn to page 3)

FIFTH DAY

Light immortal! Light Divine!
Visit Thou these hearts of Thine,
And our inmost being fill!

The Gift of Knowledge

The gift of Knowledge enables the soul to evaluate created things at their true worth—in their relation to God. Knowledge unmasks the pretense of creatures, reveals their emptiness, and points out their only true purpose as instruments in the service of God. It shows us the loving care of God even in adversity, and directs us to glorify Him in every circumstance of life. Guided by its light, we put first things first, and prize the friendship of God beyond all else. "Knowledge is a fountain of life to him that possesseth it."

Prayer

Come, O Blessed Spirit of Knowledge, and grant that I may perceive the will of the Father; show me the nothingness of earthly things, that I may realize their vanity and use them only for Thy glory and my own salvation, looking ever beyond them to Thee, and Thy eternal rewards. Amen.

Our Father and Hail Mary ONCE.
Glory be to the Father SEVEN TIMES.
Act of Consecration, Prayer for the Seven Gifts.
(Turn to page 3)

SIXTH DAY

If Thou take Thy grace away,
Nothing pure in man will stay,
All his good is turn'd to ill.

The Gift of Understanding

Understanding, as a gift of the Holy Ghost, helps us to grasp the meaning of the truths of our holy religion. By faith we know them, but by Understanding we learn to appreciate and relish them. It enables us to penetrate the inner meaning of revealed truths and through them to be quickened to newness of life. Our faith ceases to be sterile and inactive, but inspires a mode of life that bears eloquent testimony to the faith that is in us; we begin to "walk worthy of God in all things pleasing, and increasing in the knowledge of God."

Prayer

Come, O Spirit of Understanding, and enlighten our minds, that we may know and believe all the mysteries of salvation; and may merit at last to see the eternal light in Thy Light; and in the light of glory to have a clear vision of Thee and the Father and the Son. Amen.

Our Father and Hail Mary ONCE.
Glory be to the Father SEVEN TIMES.
Act of Consecration, Prayer for the Seven Gifts.
(Turn to page 3)

SEVENTH DAY

Heal our wounds—our strength renew;
On our dryness pour Thy dew;
Wash the stains of guilt away!

The Gift of Counsel

The gift of Counsel endows the soul with supernatural prudence, enabling it to judge promptly and rightly what must be done, especially in difficult circumstances. Counsel applies the principles furnished by Knowledge and Understanding to the innumerable concrete cases that confront us in the course of our daily duty as parents, teachers, public servants, and Christian citizens. Counsel is supernatural common sense, a priceless treasure in the quest of salvation. "Above all these things, pray to the Most High, that He may direct thy way in truth."

Prayer

Come, O Spirit of Counsel, help and guide me in all my ways, that I may always do Thy holy will. Incline my heart to that which is good; turn it away from all that is evil, and direct me by the straight path of Thy commandments to that goal of eternal life for which I long. Amen.

Our Father and Hail Mary ONCE.
Glory be to the Father SEVEN TIMES.
Act of Consecration, Prayer for the Seven Gifts.
(Turn to page 3)

EIGHTH DAY

Bend the stubborn heart and will;
Melt the frozen, warm the chill;
Guide the steps that go astray!

The Gift of Wisdom

Embodying all the other gifts, as charity embraces all the other virtues, Wisdom is the most perfect of the gifts. Of wisdom it is written, "all good things came to me with her, and innumerable riches through her hands." It is the gift of Wisdom that strengthens our faith, fortifies hope, perfects charity, and promotes the practice of virtue in the highest degree. Wisdom enlightens the mind to discern and relish things divine, in the appreciation of which earthly joys lose their savor, whilst the Cross of Christ yields a divine sweetness according to the words of the Saviour: "Take up thy cross and follow me, for my yoke is sweet and my burden light."

Prayer

Come, O Spirit of Wisdom, and reveal to my soul the mysteries of heavenly things, their exceeding greatness, power and beauty. Teach me to love them above and beyond all the passing joys and satisfactions of earth. Help me to attain them and possess them for ever. Amen.

Our Father and Hail Mary ONCE.
Glory be to the Father SEVEN TIMES.
Act of Consecration, Prayer for the Seven Gifts.
(Turn to page 3)

NINTH DAY

Thou, on those who evermore
Thee confess and Thee adore,
In Thy sevenfold gifts, descend:
Give them comfort when they die;
Give them life with Thee on high;
Give them joys which never end. Amen.

The Fruits of the Holy Ghost

The gifts of the Holy Ghost perfect the supernatural virtues by enabling us to practice them with greater docility to divine inspiration. As we grow in the knowledge and love of God under the direction of the Holy Ghost, our service becomes more sincere and generous, the practice of virtue more perfect. Such acts of virtue leave the heart filled with joy and consolation and are known as Fruits of the Holy Ghost. These Fruits in turn render the practice of virtue more attractive and become a powerful incentive for still greater efforts in the service of God, to serve Whom is to reign.

Prayer

Come, O Divine Spirit, fill my heart with Thy heavenly fruits, Thy charity, joy, peace, patience, benignity, goodness, faith, mildness, and temperance, that I may never weary in the service of God, but by continued faithful submission to Thy inspiration may merit to be united eternally with Thee in the love of the Father and the Son. Amen.

Our Father and Hail Mary ONCE.
Glory be to the Father SEVEN TIMES.
Act of Consecration, Prayer for the Seven Gifts.
(Turn to page 3)

Archconfraternity of the Holy Ghost

The Confraternity of the Holy Ghost was canonically established in the Chapel of the Seven Gifts of the Holy Ghost at Holy Ghost Missionary College, Cornwells Heights, Pa., on October eighth, 1912, and on June thirteenth, 1922, it was elevated to the rank of an Archconfraternity by Apostolic Letters of His Holiness, Pope Pius XI. The students who are there preparing for the missionary and apostolic life say special prayers for the intentions of the members of the Archconfraternity.

Object of the Archconfraternity

The object of the Archconfraternity is:

1. To glorify God, the Holy Ghost, and draw down His gifts upon the Church, the Sovereign Pontiff, the Bishops and the Clergy;
2. To obtain an abundance of His gifts for all, especially for the members of the Archconfraternity;

24

3. To obtain the conversion of sinners, and the
   light of faith for infidels.

For current information on the
Archconfraternity of the Holy Ghost,

Visit: http://www.spiritans.org/comm/arch.html

Call: (412) 831-0302

or

Write: Archconfraternity of the Holy Ghost
       6230 Brush Run Rd.
       Bethel Park, PA 15102

TAN · BOOKS

TAN Books was founded in 1967 to preserve the spiritual, intellectual and liturgical traditions of the Catholic Church. At a critical moment in history TAN kept alive the great classics of the Faith and drew many to the Church. In 2008 TAN was acquired by Saint Benedict Press. Today TAN continues its mission to a new generation of readers.

From its earliest days TAN has published a range of booklets that teach and defend the Faith. Through partnerships with organizations, apostolates, and mission-minded individuals, well over 10 million TAN booklets have been distributed.

More recently, TAN has expanded its publishing with the launch of Catholic calendars and daily planners—as well as Bibles, fiction, and multimedia products through its sister imprints Catholic Courses (CatholicCourses.com) and Saint Benedict Press (SaintBenedictPress.com).

Today TAN publishes over 500 titles in the areas of theology, prayer, devotions, doctrine, Church history, and the lives of the saints. TAN books are published in multiple languages and found throughout the world in schools, parishes, bookstores and homes.

For a free catalog, visit us online at
TANBooks.com

Or call us toll-free at
(800) 437-5876